The Fix

The Fix

Poems by Lisa Wells

University of Iowa Press
Iowa City

University of Iowa Press, Iowa City 52242
Copyright © 2018 Lisa Wells
www.uipress.uiowa.edu
Printed in the United States of America

Interior design by Omega Clay

The University of Iowa Press is a member of Green Press Initiative and
is committed to preserving natural resources.

Printed on acid-free paper

Library of Congress Cataloging-in-Publication Data
Names: Wells, Lisa, 1982–author.
Title: The fix : poems / by Lisa Wells.
Description: Iowa City : University of Iowa Press, [2018] | Series: Iowa
Poetry Prize
Identifiers: LCCN 2017039387| ISBN 978-1-60938-547-7 (pbk : acid-free
paper) | ISBN 978-1-60938-548-4 (ebk)
Classification: LCC PS3623.E4755 (ebk) | LCC PS3623.E4755 A6 2018
(print) |
DDC 811/.6—dc23
LC record available at https://lccn.loc.gov/2017039387

For my sister, Prudence, who opened the way

Contents

We must kill the false woman who is preventing the live one from breathing.—Hélène Cixous

I

Chore Wheel

Consulting the pie of pastels I discover
it's Monday. The garbage bin is tipped on two wheels
and driven down the walk by the grave

valet—in pajamas, pale blue silk
stuffed into my boots and zipped into the down
parka, an ambulatory cloud.

I don't care what the neighbors think.
I will meditate long on these pubic weeds
tangled on a mound of hollowing snow.

In the bedroom, the stain of last night's jag
evaporates from the pillowcase.
I am visited nightly

by a writhing.
Courtesan of the double malt,
a blear year.

Year of the drought and the vortex.
Year of my birthday (predictably).
Of the blighted ovum, I've been

dispossessed for some time now
in the street, an icy wind
bats at my drawstrings

and my hands, I notice,
are cupped, calving the light.

"Cain Flees"

the Accuser hath
Enter'd into me as into his house—William Blake

Like phantom limbs, we've learned
the source of the inner voice

is in its signal. Bantam song
    whispered in an upper chamber

while dinner resumes below.

One white plate heaped with peas,
one untouched gravy-smothered cutlet is
    conspicuously whisked from the table.

Strike a tuning fork to cancel
    voices no one else can hear—

pure tone quakes from prong to cranium

trips the neurochemical glitch.

If these transients rise oracular at their bench
if they slur against your cower

remember when you're sore afraid:
    even the prophets pissed their shifts.

No lightning strikes this deep in the field.
No tremor of bone or cochlea.

As for sight, Blake's painting sears.
                        An inner drum *dadums*.

If it's Cain who strides from Abel's corpse
hands against his temples
to stub the mother's howl

    (though the howl is *in* his house)

don't mistake him for your brother.

You are the stony garden
    where sooty clouds slide by

        and sun leaks into the firmament.

You're the trembling flame that fevered
    the flesh of Teresa Avila
        sicut infirmitas

and the *slain infant in the mother's womb*.

If the voice says you'll lie
in the indelible peace of a slaughtered dog

take her at her word.

If she says *jump bitch*:   comply.
        If she says *flee*.

Self-Portrait with Hands

after José Clemente Orozco

1.

and another drawn dog parades
on the Plaza, archipelagos of mange
gnawed across his ribs.

The girl runs her hand the length
of one mutt's spine with tremulous care
and she is the song advancing

from the bullhorn, bungeed to the roof
of the propane delivery truck, suave call
of the man repeating
    bo-ni-ta . . .

The city, wrapped in static, sings to being

   though the pistil is
twisted, painfully
pinched

bedded in broad magenta petals

the bougainvillea
blushes, labial.

Let every wound be dashed
to the hand of a woman.

2. "Hombre de Fuego"

in sepia, in coke-bottle spectacles, Orozco
scales the scaffold one-handed, frail
from rheumatic fever, toward the nude's turned heel.

Nuns flock, in habit, near my bench
to study the murdered worker's grimace
agonized in perseverating light, they carry

their own shade. For every torqued expression
in the vaultings of the nave: a blister
on the nude ascending

into the cupola.
Burned again by the young Republican
who spent her breath in my ear
all night—

how easily we flatter, humiliate,
botch the midlife crisis; snubbed by some
prima ballerina, the paintings unimproved.

Orozco knew—too much touch
gluts sensibility, and seduction's just
another stick-up

nice and slow

      come out of your lie
   with your lies up

3. "La Chata"

or get wrecked
with Giaconda Divine in the dimmest dive,
one extra white Marlboro plastered to her lip

brazenly flush with collagen—I ache
to pluck the pale finger and drag
so I guess the wine is working.

I'm fresh as a scalded babe!
Everything touches me.
Giaconda's crush on Morrissey
her baby fat, her hand

the boys delivering bowls in the Birria kitchen
with its high wall of brightly painted tile,
radiant in neon nail polish and hairnets

bearing such heavy trays,
though their arms are ropes of flame.

My god am I obvious.
Lust does not resent the lie
sweetening on this beauty's tongue

a prodigious drunk who claims
she's   *never missed anyone*
in all her twenty-one years, yet appears

to miss everything. Need, for example,
beating off in the eaves of 9 Esquinas
where the moon knuckles down

through tall palms
and each frond's edge
an immutable blade.

Lake Havasu

Detectives discovered a divot in the sapling
where the killer tested his garrote—
improvised from baling wire.

He'd been casting for necks when I stepped off
the bus this morning, moist towel of Dramamine
girding my brain. I was sitting in the Travel Center

dining room, near the wall of shotguns
and plasticized bass, when a child came to offer me
the leash of her balloon. *Lake Havasu Sunrise*

Rotary Dance & Derby. My reflection in the Mylar
and that of the girl—were bent.
I remembered you slept at a rest stop

off Hwy 40, in the backseat of your mother's car,
teeth eroded to nubs by all the scavenged
citrus fruit. I'd like to say, kissing you

stalled the *wonder if*
my mouth could bear its own endurance. I'm sorry
I mistook you for a killer. All my life

I've been confused. A man moves his quaking hand
inside my tights and weeps. Don't like the thing he does
but I eat the Poptart after.

Outside this window, boats stock
the reservoir with carp. Heavy rigging drags
the aqueduct for evidence.

Theory of Knowledge

Alive on the highway shoulder.
The ruddy trucker passed

tossed a can from his cab
and I scrambled to retrieve it.

Cut like a twig and titless
the boys said
bbs on a breadboard.

Crossed my arms over my chest
in the frigid stock room of the mini-mart
while a classmate donned a nylon bib
and counted my cache into his hamper.

So I whipped a boy at school with my windbreaker
and where my zipper caught his shin, he split.

Blood slipped through the fold
mercury slow.

For that, a teacher faced me toward a wall
to think about my wrongs.

I don't need a wall to know.

Saddle Shoes

We circled in the bedroom of the trailer
and passed a can of Spring Rain Glade.

Our careful mouths stretched over the nozzle,
washcloth between, we huffed deep the clouds.

I lay back on the bed expanding,
pathetic with pleasure

and stared at a poster of a kitten
in bobby socks and saddle shoes.

The good god placed that kitten in my eye,
coated my bones in baby fat

but could not spare me the fingers
of fatherless boys.

The prettiest of us had babies
with three different dads, she manages

an all night IHOP off the interstate.
Once, I watched her descend a stair

in a strapless dress, the delicate
sleigh of her clavicle caught

the light of a naked bulb
and I prayed to god   *Please let me be her*

and the god of the refried cigarette
the No-Doz overdose

in his singular mercy
didn't answer.

1989

Roused on the isthmus dividing eastbound
and westbound, launched from the grill
of an '86 Cutlass, wicked knot throbbing

on my crown. I remember the driver
swerving. I stood absolutely still. Ascension
omitted. That frame's been clipped

along with the wire joining
input and animal fear. It was
the year I attempted to defect

to the lion enclosure, stuck neck-deep in the bars
the pride stirred, rose upon their haunches.
25 years they've stalked from shade

in my mind's eye. *What a difference a foot makes*
notes the near-death recidivist
budged to the edge

of the subway platform.
When the ravening out of darkness speeds
and the bad star advances in the channel

one eye looks inside, one away.
To step or lapse to the flesh?
No one is coming

to slather my head in margarine
and slip me back to my keeper's hands.

"Woman Seated with Thighs Apart"

after Klimt

Often I am permitted to return to this kitchen
tipsy, pinned to the fridge, to the precise
instant the kiss smashed in.

When the jaws of night are grinding
and the double bed is half asleep

the snore beside me syncs
to the traffic light, pulsing red, ragged up
in the linen curtain.

I leak such solicitous sighs
to asphalt, slicked with black ice, high beams speed
over my body whole

while the drugstore weeps its remedy
in strident neon throbs—
I doubt I'll make it out.

It's a cold country. It's the sting of quarantine.
It's my own two hands working
deep inside the sheets.

Up

No more infinite opening.
The winter holds
fast to the blustered hedges.
On a clear day
the sun seems remote
and flayed, the ghosts
high cirrus streak. Sweet
Galina, the distance splices her scene
into my strip: in the black-lit
bathroom of the club
our nostrils slid a track
to charisma, powder flared
in the vacuum—
I hoisted her bare ass
to the titanium shelf
and nudged apart her knees.
Into the witless dim
I go, into my own
development
where a wayward Ruffles bag
wefts desiccated grass.
The sensual world
builds cells in the mind
—false paneled, hatched,
the tongue and groove
limns my limits.

I don't grow, anymore,
by the inch. I gain
ground. I tone down
the stimulants.

II

The Fix

I go get this diagnosis.

Symptoms to order
the affect.

Deep in my circadian clock
the seasons wheel
but something stays

displaced.
A fingernail.
A tangle of hair in the leaf litter.

Cardinals, ganged up in oaks,
bob their tweaker skulls,
unleash alarms—

The fix will not get in me.

To be or blank
the brain. Vain to dream
that violence.

To unite us.
You know you

snuff one self
but the urge continues,
jumps down like fleas

from dog to dog.

Better to go on   I read
in the book I took from mother.

Mother, in your hands
my head
is not such bad creation.

I mean, the fault's not
in your fingers.

If I could just retrace
my steps and

find the fix.
Knock it in me.

Canis Vulgaris

Sallow, furred, I wore my sores.
Nightmare of sebum

wake in aching cysts. Insist on oil-free,
cream of sulfur, decongest my angry liver

nothing makes it better.

In the myth, The Rough Faced Girl
levels clear as glass, achieves a husband.

Moral is: the out reflects the in.
Don't need a mirror to know.

I keep clean, enraged, rough bitch in me
clicks her claws, swipes and overtakes

the pretty little things.

Instructions

If it's blanched and fat with fluid
drop your pick and puncture it.
Stake it through the mouth.
Unsocket and incinerate its heart.
If any home is plagued, nurse each sick
two spoons of ash. If it's rotted, if
it bears no bloody beard
fold inside its ear a note of absolution.
Consecrate a brick
to stretch inside its cheeks.
Hook a silver blade behind
the tendons of each knee. Unstringed,
she'll not rise again. Scatter grains of millet
to fill her idle hours—vain, compulsive
accountant of coin and compliment—
she counts. Overturn the box
spill her to the dirt. Strip her. Switch her.
Take this wild rose. Here, take this
Hawthorn branch and lash her naked buttocks.
Purse her in a pack of wild pig.
Disconnect her head
and plug it between her ankles.
Stomp her with a boot.
Light the linen shroud,
club it as it burns, and laugh
and piss on it.

Memoir

I stitched my mask of hide- snout- sinew- talon- and rode
the vast savanna to war

in my former life. I was the hybrid. I sewed my brutal double-helix
    into a child

and packed her boots with greasy wool that felted as she walked in bright

stratified color. Carpathian bronze couldn't buy her off
when she leapt at the throat of my lover.

Him I called The Lion for his yawn and yellow ringlets.

I placed a Deglet date upon his tongue, I pressed
the golden scarab into amber, straddled all his lap, kissed

my cresset to the yurts of my superiors

and in this life, I think I'd like to do more damage.

Object Relations

brushed up on some supernal
sublimation. An asteroid

is falling toward the planet
packed in ice

big as a big building
reports the flustered analyst.

~

it's little old me: the dream of the grunt
who flexed in cathedrals of concrete

who deafened in
hydraulic hush

to bring home the bacon
and Oleoline.

~

for my forbear labored deep
in a hospital basement

fed biohazards to an incinerator.

Objects issued from the hole,
unidentified

bodies above—revised,
bagged and vanished

down a blind aluminum chute
to his hands.

~

his hands that gripped
the hips that dropped

the egg that met
the fish that struck

the match in me

I'm burning

and they say the rock will miss
the earth, but just.

Refusal Studies

The Ocean

did not "break."
It was not empty.
Crystal stemware slipped

into the sink
nicked this
scattershot of blood across

my fingers' webbing.
Irradiated wreckage slams
the sand at Pacific City

every hour the news
wraiths through the radio.
I'm not sure we're capable

of rescue.
Tide drags flotsam deep
into the cave where

shadow chills the pale forms.
Can't get warm.

The Anthropocene

will conclude in the forests of Ecuador;
in block 31;   in one densely tangled hectare;
in a hut   half thatched   half
corrugated steel;   in the spear
driven in the eye of the elder: signifier
for liar.

why beholdest thou the mote
            in thy brother's eye?   Oh me

   of little faith;   little
lamb;   locust
            on which the gentle Baptist dined.

In Iowa, I lay
a pebble in the inroad

every time I *fill 'er up*
vigorously rub my mitts, but not for glee.

The Cochin Cockerel

strung up by the shanks, will not say
who's guilty.

One hand pins his wings to his breast
while the other draws the blade

drains his thrash into a blue
plastic bucket.

Spinning, blood-spattered
ballerino in my arms

I gather him again, his umber cape
warm in my palm,
fight jerked out.

Dependably, a hood is cinched
to cover the broken gaze

bound wrist to wrist
pulse to pulse

the scaffold pledges sleep
but the feet dance on
in the clatter.

Resurrections

We lived on earth, were prone to pack
like dogs, my friends and me.

We die like dogs while milk sings
in somebody else's mouth.

You want to talk about redemption?
Go tell it to heaven

freezing in space. Tell the Father
with his hopeless charge—*Heal the sick*

Raise the dead
I am a beast

there's a wound in me
and everyone knows

you should never trust
what comes to you limping.

Revelations

Now that the gods are limping
in knotted cord and ring of thorns,
psalms reduced to mournful aluminum
160 BPM—Now that I'm shaking
in the tachycardic chatter of gun belts
emptying, a snub-nosed .357
snug against my rib—Now that the growl's begun
in the subwoofer, the spoiler, the sun's
magma tongues lashing *horror vacui*—I see
the light-bars are on and the boys are out
fourbying tonight, hollering *GET SOME*
tossing the empties over. Their faces simple
as the hill at Golgotha, their smiles
cracking through. One of them says
he wants *in* me, it's that easy: any wound
will do. The moon gone. The hour late.

Someone rolls the boulder back.
We kill the engine and wait.

Revelations II

In the logical library, in the steady hands of science
I circle the stacks, abstracted. Some innovations
pollute the mind, send the soul skittering
to shade. Observe the caged girls
stroked by truckers hauling long
out of Kelso. The habit of kerosene to glow
romantic. Disfigured honey. Enter my eyes.
These lines stack up like bodies.
Salted with bullets. Chained.
The dozers never doze, the misery-whips
lockstep, advancing, salmon fat with egg
skirt Grand Coulee, drape the bank's
red willow, gray and moth-eaten these
discarded rags. Still dream of a world
where life can happen.

Didn't motor oil smear that rainbow in me?
This mercury, rising
inside my sights
so I will see
my most heroic gesture
cannot hope to keep
any living thing I love alive.

BEAST

for Sean Anderson

1.

I've come to kneel
on the filthy kitchen floor
of the punk squat.

The girl you were sleeping with
has a beautiful face
and a booze-fat mouth.

She cracks can after can of Pabst,
rhapsodizes on the silver-lined
caesura of your pain.

//

You have given us this
broken neck, suspended flesh

refusal looped between
like a short wave beacon *not Sean*

a record turns and turns
beneath the noose

though the needle rests
and no music threads through.

Sink
Like a Symphony
reads the sleeve.

2.

In the park adjacent the crematory
there is a toddler
hidden in the folds of her stroller.

Only her hands are visible
kneading the air.

I spot you, crossing the lawn
in your polyester slacks
and wave.

Forget your body laid
at the iron gate,
sheet tugged up to your chin.

Your mother and an orderly shoving you in.

Rush of white fire in the chambered cochlea.
Your mother falling back into my arms

slowly
as if through water

and the flies droning
in between the window's glass and screen

have each
a thousand eyes.

Fire the chimneys. Rise
from your burning turret

come outside.

3.

Your double crosses the lawn
and squinting lifts
his hand to block the sun.

I am your mother now
in the screen door
the man saluting

bearing the bad news
of his body. Not yours.

Sink like a symphony

and the children shake their fists.
The flowers fall apart.

4.

I drive home.
I make a pizza.
Raise the dough,
grate the cheese, lay down
green leaves of fragrant basil.
Eat.

I undress my husband.
Take him in my mouth,
his mouth on my mouth,
pull him inside me.

I prove we breathe.

5.

Whatever relief promised
by the drunken impulse, may it come.

To ash, to earth, to urn
interred to the cardboard box
—ash is hardly anything.

To the tightly wound stem
pushing through dark earth

unfurling when finally you feel the sun

but if instead
of the white hallway,
figure of love embodied

you meet only the vacuum you left,
an unthinking void

then all the better.

III

Resurrections II

A seed sleeps till you put it in the ground.
A seed is a box water opens.

I bend over the dirt
repeating the names

and feel them on their way back to me
busting their husks, rushing to surface.

If they can't come back I'll whimper.
Beast at the tree line, pacing.

If they can't come
I'm a set of teeth.
A hollow growl.

"Under the Water, Carry the Water"

after Talking Heads

If there is weeping in this place, no one hears.

All the riding mowers going and the men
astride their machines, float along the lawns
with princely composure.

I am alive in the house each night and so
I sense the grasses straining

       they throb and they extend.

I loved my husband best when he was spent,
slicked with sweat, delivered shirtless
from the yard.

Here, an outside man is paid to do it

and there is time to observe
the churn

of rotors
roaring in my forehead.

To endure this
apparatus

all I have to do is last.

~

Morning came and came
again, I rose

put coffee on and waited

in the bathtub
while the water flowed

loathed and craved what most
I needed

man in my kitchen
hardly known, hardly knows

the water holds me down.
Born again

from a lukewarm rill
an inner counsel warns

there may be some discomfort
in taking other forms.

Yank the plug—funnel touches down
sounds the suction.

Which way it came or where
the water goes

I couldn't say.

~

He often brought me flowers.

I thought of their struggle
from burial to the thin

air of the world
into color

how they were severed,
scattered across our table

the calm unraveled
the mind pursued its dim

circle of light to meaning
  everything ends.

He married a mind like that.
Like a mole

dark and small

but tenacious.
Undermining every happy lawn.

~

Wake to touch the potted earth,
gauge its moisture, the spring
in the fronds, feel for rot.

I have a feel for it.

I have forfeited his hands
moonrise in the ridged nails
carbide band.

In sleep
he bucked with dreams
he stole the sheet

all the hours we shared a bed

now night song leaks into my ears unchanged

        it rings within
      the gutted room
   you lose

and the platitude is true: life goes on

it goes and goes

The Hitch

There is a kink in the cure. —T. Murray

not sex—intercession of flesh—
not communion in a body

not faithful but still slip
into the dim, confess

I failed to grasp the Who,
which venial wrong would deal

the mortal blow. The psalm was
unremarkable, save:

every warm-blooded creature contains
brains enough to tan its own hide

why those suits keep coming back
from the discard pile to haunt us

we don't do right by what's in hand
disclosure, contrition, amends

marching bead by worried bead
upon my rosary—fails to reconcile

a knot in the garland
that keeps on hitching

---   ---   ---   ---

who can track the days

the name of the lake—
what music played

the way the waves reached out
withdrew and

insect-chorus scored
the summer dark—

the night we drunk on Mickey's Fine
lukewarm malt liquor

watched the water mount and fold
and fucked each other—

of memory, I'm a simple girl—
easy to please short-term

at present I wonder when you'll come round
to overturn this

remember—   recover your—
metronomic wah—my One

what warped-platter spun
the white-vinyl

with a diamond stylus hitching

---   ---   ---   ---

and an itch in it
real bad

I'm ringing like an apse oh

lay your pick, I'll break
and spill the shades

the ornate agate aches,
silk against the bone—

to pity the need you must
punish the stone

spare the strop: spoil the grovel
—speak the *please*

all tongues contain. Cannot
contain. The *please*

erupting in my face—
in lust, or blissed, or anguished

at the wrist
by rod, by riding crop

divined—you love a dim
shaft in collapse, where daylight

rushed to stitch the gash
you have me

on my knees now
    cleave your woman.

The earth moves—

We Must Be Coming Down

for we feel the subcutaneous lace
of strychnine unstitching in fitful
intervals. Once awash in tracers—nested
parentheses—yield now to the muted
sitcom in the TV room. I reached into
the interstice between the loveseat
and La-Z-Boy to touch your hand.
You have kept me, so successfully
from mirrors, where the peaking stand
to vanish, examining illusory blemishes.
This sickness is peripheral. It dodges
the dead-on gaze like the glancing
stars. I woke from thought's collapsing
inside my own pupil, blown, wormhole
to the soul, sorry for all I've said aloud.

Repairing the Flat

Bike, ride me tonight
beyond this sleepy grid

of grain—tassel-heads tower
in rows, robed in silk and heavy

professorial silence.
Teeth concealed.

I have to peddle hard.
Drivers try to run me over.

Nothing personal.

A man lies awake in a bitter bed
spending, in his mind, his tardy MacArthur.

Only his penis sleeps.
It cowers against the crepe of his thigh

recoils to a white bramble
with a bad dream.

Dream of the girlfriend's knee,
the zipper teeth.

Dream of the ornery Quarter Horse.
Everyone that hurt him.

Monday Night at the Pagoda

Then we're at the bar again, lit
by the poker machine's thin light, drop ceiling
breathing overhead, discussing your heart attack
—harmonic scalpel deployed to the blue
river where they split you stalk to thigh.
I order whiskey, close my eyes
around the first warm measures and ride
the surgeon's tackle through the dark
of your pelvis, kingdom of chest.

When they open I call out for another
tumbler and the bartender turns away
her blue-veined mask in disgust. She knows
I'm going to give it up
in the empty parking lot, the static cab
of your truck. Tonight
your pulse blinks steady as an eye
and you are nowhere near it.

State of a Fair

Pig trough says, spill your trouble here.
Allow these candy clouds to cotton
the sting.

    Your man's a sad balloon

and love was an afternoon hovered over
the whack-a-mole. It was precisely that

systematic vanishing
gave rise to the rubber mallet

and four fat knuckles
rapped on wood.

If you don't know what to do now
with your hands, consider the terror

pealing from the coasters.
    Descent demands you stick-em-up.

    Metal splinter glints
above, sun-struck jet slicing the ether
        completely free to travel

from the turbulence,
   inveigled to stay aloft
      on fair-weather prayer.

      Dear bright lure
   softly bobbing on the void,
spare us this stick

of deep fried butter, this pie-spiked shake.
Our tickers can only take so much.

The children comfort their cones
with such gentle tongues

you'd think the ice cream was injured.
Scant tantrums in this

   queue. Our helices unspool
but no life's long enough to host the evolution

and no one's stepping out of line.
When enervation strikes, just lid your eyes

and apply an ounce of pressure:
you can visit space any time you like.

Winemaking

Slide the cork from the bottle and a song
like the first sun of summer ripples through
my skin, makes me lie down in warm water.

Or else a minor chord commands I grip
the railing of the Broadway Bridge
and beg the moon

full as a grape. The wine's a risk
I'll have to take. Every day
learning how little I know

how young and afraid.
Atrophied the muscle
required to say *mortgage*

how casually the panicked
incantation is spoken—
like we'll never die.

Truth is, I'm not young at all.
I may be more than half expired.
An afternoon. A papery cask

and two orbs of desiccating eggs.
When you think of it that way
don't I deserve another drink?

Come, boy. Bring your bottle.
Bat your lashes. Show me that
smile you practiced with all your teeth.

The night is a vascular bundle, sealed
in tight skin. The world a vineyard of blue
chandeliers when the music begins.

"Poetry Man"

after Phoebe Snow

To recall the cull of this life.

That one must harvest by selective annulment
the body they will wed

        and the body they will hustle
from dress to tongue on the sly

              for days
I lay as a flank in my lover's maw

        swathed in wine while warm
winds frisked the wisteria.

It was innocent.

He lashed my wrist to the mast.
He tied my blind because I wanted

to be battered in the swell
    and blossoms purple still
any place he pressed his mouth
any place

I asked for it.
By now I know, I begged:
relieve your mouth its bland aperture

Talk to me some more.

~

Home's that place   somewhere   you go each day

In absence of his finger I have conveyed to my teeth
a relentless procession of corn chips, zoned out

on the bedroom wall.
Little my tongue does for the hole it circumnavigates.

It was a clear day, sun jigging figures from the leaves
on the alien green of College Park
        I was ocular in his arms

an enormous pupil, blown open.

    We knew the hour had come
by the way the light collected

raptured to several heavens
there's no need to choose.

~

If choice is obviated   "Le Paradis n'est pas artificiel"

his letter begins, anxiety of what is
in back of each long note.

He compares me to a garden   "Why weed what winter will kill?"

Fidelity is perennial, survives the cold   cloaked as a peony.

He wishes me a grand carouse at the local dive, a dry
bottom bun for my rubber burger
and another man's sex   *bashful boy*.

~

do not touch the stove you will

fuse to its element   slaver over
the burn.   *You don't have to go.*

You're hiding something sweet
from this swollen thumb

and from these glossy welts derives
the suspicion that I am truly sick.

Monstrously wooed by these
reports of injury, he admits

    "its invocation of parts. You have a thumb. Eyes."

Instruments of agency.   Logic divides
pleasure from having
    give it to me

All Medea's remonstrations ended on a blade,
downed in the poisoned mug, draped in the tainted gown

but she never howled
when love departed

she muscled out to meet him.

Acknowledgments

Thanks to the editors of the following publications where these poems first appeared, sometimes in different forms: *Denver Quarterly, Blackbird, The Iowa Review, Best New Poets 2014, Poor Claudia (First Floor), Hazlitt, OmniVerse, Inter/rupture, The Rumpus, Plazm Magazine, Dunes Review, Coldfront, Southern Humanities Review,* and *Prelude.* Several of these poems were first collected in the chapbook *BEAST* (Bedouin Books, 2012).

I'm grateful to those who bettered the poems and/or the poet: Mark Levine, D. A. Powell, Richard Kenney, Ted Mathys, Davy Knittle, Daniel Poppick, Kazim Ali, Nikki-Lee Birdsey, Jessica Laser, Christian Schlegel, Jake Fournier, Grant Souders, Micah Bateman, Brit Washburn, Caitlin Roach, Nick Bozanic, and W. E. Butts. Thanks to my family and to my chosen family in Portland. I'm especially grateful to those who helped keep my head in the zip code while writing these poems: Timothy Kelly, Yael Podebski, Zaina Arafat, and Zach Savich. Thanks also to Mary Hickman, Ariel Lewiton, Ian Miller, Julia Whicker, Charles D'Ambrosio, Julia Ain Krupa, Margaret Ross, Jay Nebel, Dot Devota, Brandon Shimoda, Brenda Hillman, Jane Miller, and Rob and Sue Rea for your friendship and support.

I owe a debt to the Vermont Studio Center, The Sou'wester, and The Iowa Writers' Workshop (Jan, Deb, Kelly, and Connie) for time and space to work.

Finally, to Joshua Marie Wilkinson: thank you. For the long conversation. For finding me on the other side.

"Cain Flees" is after the pen and ink by William Blake. "Self-Portrait with Hands" is after works by José Clemente Orozco. "Woman Seated with Thighs Apart" is after the Gustav Klimt painting. "Instructions" compiles advice shared during the New England vampire panic of the late nineteenth century. In "BEAST," *Sink Like a Symphony* is quoted from the Fred Thomas record by the same name. "Poetry Man" is the title of a song by Phoebe Snow.

Iowa Poetry Prize and Edwin Ford Piper Poetry Award Winners

1987   Elton Glaser, *Tropical Depressions*
        Michael Pettit, *Cardinal Points*

1988   Bill Knott, *Outremer*
        Mary Ruefle, *The Adamant*

1989   Conrad Hilberry, *Sorting the Smoke*
        Terese Svoboda, *Laughing Africa*

1990   Philip Dacey, *Night Shift at the Crucifix Factory*
        Lynda Hull, *Star Ledger*

1991   Greg Pape, *Sunflower Facing the Sun*
        Walter Pavlich, *Running near the End of the World*

1992   Lola Haskins, *Hunger*
        Katherine Soniat, *A Shared Life*

1993   Tom Andrews, *The Hemophiliac's Motorcycle*
        Michael Heffernan, *Love's Answer*
        John Wood, *In Primary Light*

1994   James McKean, *Tree of Heaven*
        Bin Ramke, *Massacre of the Innocents*
        Ed Roberson, *Voices Cast Out to Talk Us In*

1995   Ralph Burns, *Swamp Candles*
        Maureen Seaton, *Furious Cooking*

1996   Pamela Alexander, *Inland*
        Gary Gildner, *The Bunker in the Parsley Fields*
        John Wood, *The Gates of the Elect Kingdom*

1997   Brendan Galvin, *Hotel Malabar*
        Leslie Ullman, *Slow Work through Sand*